Twenty Texans

Historic Lives for Young Readers

Twenty Texans

Historic Lives for Young Readers

Written and Illustrated

by

Betsy Warren

Hendrick-Long Publishing Company

Dallas

Library of Congress Cataloging-in-Publication Data

Warren, Betsy.
　　　Twenty Texans.

　　　Summary: Biographies of twenty men and women in Texan history, from the Mexican rebel Lorenzo de Zavala to the politician Barbara Jordan.
　　　1. Texas—Biography—Juvenile literature. [I. Texas—Biography] I. Title.
CT262.W37　1985　976.4′009′92 [B] [920]　　　85-13926
ISBN 0-937460-17-6

ISBN 1-885777-08-6 (pb)
ISBN 0-937460-17-6 (hb)

Copyright © 1985 Hendrick-Long Publishing Company
Dallas, TX 75225

Table of Contents

Lorenzo de Zavala

1788-1836

Learned Rebel From Mexico

There was no school in the tiny village of Tecoh, Mexico, where Lorenzo de Zavala was born. When he was old enough, his parents sent him to a boarding school in the nearby town of Mérida. The school was run by Franciscan priests who were fine scholars.

The priests found that Lorenzo was an eager student. He liked to write, to study, and to think. In time, Lorenzo could speak and write eight languages. With little trouble, he passed courses in religion, Latin, mathematics, and philosophy.

But one thing did not come easily to Lorenzo. He could not obey rules or laws that he felt were wrong. He would give good reasons for being against them. The habit of speaking up for fairer laws stayed with him for the rest of his life.

By the time Lorenzo finished school at nineteen, he had grown so tall that he stood out among his countrymen. All over his home province of Yucatán, people knew Lorenzo de Zavala. They knew he cared deeply about how his country was governed. Over and over he declared that the people, not a king, should decide a country's laws.

At that time, the country of Mexico with its province of

1

2

Texas had belonged to Spain for almost three hundred years. Spanish kings made laws and appointed officials to rule Mexico. The king's officials did not like what Lorenzo was saying, and put him in prison. However, during the three years he spent there, Lorenzo wasted no time. He studied medicine and learned the English language.

After his release in 1817, Lorenzo practiced medicine for a short time. But it was not long before he spoke up for better laws again. Fortunately, a new king in Spain was interested in what Lorenzo had to say. During a visit with the king, Lorenzo heard the news that Mexico had received its independence from Spain on February 8, 1821.

"At last," said Lorenzo, "we will be free to govern ourselves."

He hurried home to represent Yucatán as a senator in the new Congress that met in Mexico City. With great enthusiasm, he took part in making a new constitution for the country. Writers of this constitution were known as Federalists. Lorenzo was the first to sign the document.

Not everyone in Mexico agreed with the constitution or with Lorenzo de Zavala. The opponents, called Centralists, did not want people to elect their own officials. Also, they did not like it when Lorenzo said that the province of Texas should be allowed to rule itself. The Centralists chased Lorenzo out of office as governor of the state of Mexico. To avoid being captured, Lorenzo had to hide in the hills for a month.

Gathering an army, Lorenzo and the Federalists marched back to Mexico City and defeated the Centralists. Lorenzo was given back the job of governor, and was also made Minister of the Treasury. But soon he was forced to leave again.

Taking his family, Lorenzo traveled to the United States. He met President John Quincy Adams and talked to government leaders. Following that, he went to France and wrote a book in Paris about revolutions in Mexico. When Federalists gained power in Mexico once more, Lorenzo went home.

The new Mexican president Santa Anna appointed Lorenzo minister to France. With his family, Lorenzo went back to Paris. To his great disappointment, he soon learned that Santa Anna had betrayed the Mexican people. Instead of allowing them more rights, he had become a dictator. He made all decisions for Mexico and did not listen to anyone else.

From Paris, Lorenzo wrote an angry letter to Santa Anna and resigned from the government. After deciding to live in Texas, he built a home for his family on Buffalo Bayou near Houston. When he arrived in July 1835, Lorenzo learned that William Travis had just driven Mexican soldiers from the town of Anahuac. He heard that Stephen Austin had been jailed for more than a year in Mexico City. This was because officials suspected that he was planning a break between Texas and Mexico.

Now Lorenzo was determined that the people of Texas resist Santa Anna. He traveled to all the towns and talked to the leaders.

"Don't delay," he warned. "You must act quickly to gain

liberty. Santa Anna will never give you your rights."

Some people did not want to fight Mexico. They liked and respected Lorenzo, but they did not agree with him. However, it made them angry when they heard that Santa Anna wanted them to arrest Lorenzo. "We will not give up any man in Texas to Mexican soldiers," they said.

In September 1835 Stephen Austin returned to his home in San Felipe. When he met Lorenzo de Zavala, he liked and trusted him. He believed that Lorenzo would help Texas fight Mexico for its freedom.

On February 28, 1836, Lorenzo met with fifty-eight leaders of Texas at Washington-on-the-Brazos. He helped them write down reasons to declare independence and guided them in planning a military defense. The men chose David G. Burnet as president of the temporary wartime government. Every man there cast his vote for Lorenzo de Zavala as vice-president. Later, during one of their meetings, they learned that Santa Anna was in Bastrop with his army, on the way to capture them.

With President Burnet and the other leaders, Lorenzo fled to Harrisburg. Santa Anna chased them with only a small part of his army. The Texans barely escaped to Galveston Island. Santa Anna thought he had trapped the Texans on the island. With his men, he camped in a meadow at San Jacinto to wait for the rest of his forces to arrive. General Sam Houston chose this time to lead the Texas army in an attack. In a short battle, the Mexicans were defeated on April 21, 1836.

After the defeat of his old enemy, Lorenzo was not feeling well. Still, he had agreed to escort Santa Anna back to Mexico. However, angry Texans would not let Santa Anna board the boat going to Mexico. They kept him in Texas for several months first. Lorenzo then returned to his home on Buffalo Bayou to rest.

In November, he took one of his children canoeing on the bayou. The boat overturned. Lorenzo saved his child and swam to shore in the chilling water. Illness developed, causing his death on November 15, 1836. He was buried at his home, which overlooks the battleground at San Jacinto.

In the years that followed, Texans gave many tributes to Lorenzo de Zavala. They named schools and a town after him, as well as the state archives building in Austin. It was their way of honoring the man who dared to speak out for the cause of freedom.

Stephen F. Austin

1793-1836

Scholar Who Tamed a Wilderness

Modern Texans called Stephen F. Austin the "Father of Texas." However, the first man to bring families from the United States to settle the land of this state was born in Virginia, on November 3, 1793.

When Stephen was five years old, he rode in a covered wagon and on river barges as his family moved to southern Missouri. His father, Moses Austin, opened a lead mine, mills, and a store in the small settlement of Potosi.

At first, the business was a success. Moses was able to send Stephen to schools in Connecticut and Kentucky. After two years at Transylvania College in Kentucky, Stephen returned home at the age of seventeen. He was needed to help his father with the store and mining business.

Moses asked his son to take a cargo of lead on a barge down the Mississippi River. The lead was to be sold to make bullets needed by the United States. Americans were fighting England in the War of 1812.

As the barge floated close to New Orleans, a violent storm came up. The barge and all the lead on it sank. River men told Stephen he would never be able to raise it. But Stephen waited patiently several weeks for the rain to stop and the

water to get lower. Then he and his men worked hard with ropes and levers to raise the barge. The lead was carried on to New Orleans and sold.

After returning to Missouri, Stephen gained valuable experience in lawmaking. In July 1820, he was appointed as a judge in the Arkansas Territory. In December that same year, he went to New Orleans to study law with Judge Hawkins, a man who had befriended him.

Meanwhile in Missouri, Moses Austin's lead mining business had failed. However, Moses had heard that Spain would give land in Texas to people who settled there. Moses tried to interest his son in joining him to find colonists. Stephen was not eager, but he agreed to help his father. Then suddenly, Moses died while Stephen was on his way to Texas.

Stephen chose to carry on his father's work. He explored the prairies, forests, and rivers of East Texas. A group of men from Mexico City came to help him select two hundred thousand acres for the new settlers. When Stephen talked with them and saw the fertile land, he became enthusiastic about his father's dream.

After three months, he went back to the United States. By this time, the land he had chosen was a part of Mexico, since Mexico had just won its freedom from Spain. In New Orleans, Stephen spoke to crowds of United States citizens.

"Mexico's new rulers will give thousands of acres to people who will settle in Texas," he said. "The land has great forests, is fertile and well watered. It will make excellent farms. For those who are willing to become Mexican citizens and to work hard, it is a fine opportunity."

News of Stephen's offer spread quickly. Families from many southern states put their belongings in covered wagons and moved to Texas, settling between the Brazos and Colorado rivers.

The American colonists quickly built log cabins and planted crops. Their settlement was called San Felipe de Austin. Stephen surveyed their land and kept records of each family's grant. He gave the colonists seeds and tools to start their farms.

In a short time, Mexican officials sent a message to Stephen. They said that the land had been granted by Spain to his father Moses, not to him. He would have to come to Mexico City to straighten out matters with the new Mexican government.

Traveling by horseback, Stephen began the nine-hundred-mile trip. Nineteen days later, he arrived in Mexico City. He had to wait eight months before any officials would agree to see him.

While waiting, Stephen spent his time usefully. He learned to speak Spanish, and made friends with the Mexican people. At last, the Mexican government gave him permission to manage his Texas colony. They also said he could bring more settlers into Texas and give forty-six hundred acres of land to each family.

After having been gone one year, Stephen hurried back to Texas with the good news. But the news was not good at San Felipe. Crops had failed, and Indians had raided farms and stolen horses. Many discouraged settlers had gone back to the United States.

Stephen brought seeds from San Antonio and helped the people plant new crops. He met with Indian tribes and made peace with them. He also wrote laws, while the people elected officials to enforce them in the new settlements. After seven more years of hard work, Stephen knew the colony was a success.

Troubles came again in the 1830's. Mexico had sent soldiers to Texas and would not allow the settlers to have guns. They required the settlers to pay taxes but would not let them take part in making laws. In 1833 the colonists asked Stephen to go to Mexico City again. This time they wanted him to ask that Texas have its own state government.

When Stephen reached Mexico City he became ill with cholera. After he recovered, he received permission from President Santa Anna to make reforms in Texas government. On his way home, he was arrested in Saltillo, taken back to Mexico City, and locked in an old jail. Stephen could not understand why he was in jail or why no one was allowed to speak to him.

For more than a year, Stephen was confined in Mexico. The government thought he was trying to free Texas completely from Mexican rule. Finally a new law, passed in 1835, released all prisoners in Mexico. Stephen started for home again. He had been away for two years.

Back in San Felipe, Stephen did not enjoy peace and rest for long. The Texans were now declaring that they would fight to be free from Mexico. Money was needed for soldiers and supplies, so Stephen traveled to New York to borrow from bankers there. While he was away, the Mexican army killed many Texans at Goliad and the Alamo and burned the town of Harrisburg. But at San Jacinto on April 21, 1836, the Texans defeated Santa Anna and the Mexican soldiers. Texas was now free from Mexico.

Once the war was over, people in Texas formed their own country, the Republic of Texas. They chose the town of Columbia for their capital and elected Sam Houston as president. President Houston asked Stephen Austin to be the first secretary of state in Texas.

All of San Felipe had been burned during the war. Stephen dreamed of going home to build a new house. He even sent seeds to his sister and her children so they could start the planting on his farm before he returned. He never got there.

At Christmastime in 1836, he became ill. In the cabin of of a friend in Columbia, he lay on a pallet by the fireplace. He died on December 27 and was buried at Peach Point, the plantation home of his sister Emily.

Texans did not forget Stephen F. Austin when they made their final choice of a capital. The tiny settlement of Waterloo was renamed Austin in honor of the man who had shown the Texans so much loyalty and devotion.

Sam Houston

1793-1863

Colorful Commander-in-Chief

Two horse-drawn wagons rattled through the Great Smoky Mountains in 1807. They carried the family and belongings of Mrs. Elizabeth Houston, a widow from Virginia. She was on her way to make a home on land near Knoxville, Tennessee.

With help from her five sons and three daughters, Mrs. Houston built a log home and a successful farm. All of the children shared the chores except Sam, the youngest boy. He preferred to sit under a tree and read a book. By the time he was fourteen, he had read his favorite book so often that he knew it by heart. It was *The Iliad*, a story of Greek heroes who had fought bravely in great battles of long ago.

When his brothers scolded him for wasting time, Sam ran away. He walked fifty miles to the Tennessee River and paddled a canoe out to the island of Hiwassie. For three years Sam lived with the Cherokees. Chief John Jolly adopted him as a son and named him "The Raven." To the Indians, the raven meant good fortune.

When he was twenty, Sam left the Cherokees and joined the United States Army. Under General Andrew Jackson, Sam fought in battles with Creek Indians who were attack-

14

ing white families in Alabama. After President James Monroe asked him to be an agent to the Cherokees, Sam went back to Hiwassie Island. "Your braves will be killed by the white man if they stay here," Sam told them. Chief John Jolly sadly agreed to move to Arkansas Territory.

When Sam left the army in 1817 he studied law, doing eighteen months work in six months time. After passing exams, he practiced law in Lebanon, Tennessee.

Wherever he went, Sam attracted attention. He was six feet and four inches tall, and stood very straight like an Indian. Sometimes he wore a bright blanket and beaded moccasins. People in Tennessee liked his picturesque ways. In 1827, they made him governor of their state.

Because of a failed marriage, Sam resigned as governor. He left Tennessee and traveled to the Arkansas Territory to live with the Cherokees. Chief John Jolly welcomed him again as a son. Sam put on his Indian clothes and spoke no English for the next three years.

When he saw how his Indian friends were often cheated by white men, Sam became angry. He went to Washington, D.C., to talk to the president, his old friend Andrew Jackson. President Jackson promised to help.

The president also asked Sam to visit a new colony that was being settled by families from the United States. The colony was in a vast area called Texas. President Jackson hoped to buy Texas from Mexico and to make it a part of the United States.

Sam was eager to go to Texas. Returning to Arkansas, he told his Indian friends goodbye and rode south. On December 2, 1832, Sam crossed the Red River into northeast Texas. Then he rode south to San Felipe, the center of the colony of Americans. The vast space and beautiful land made Sam want to live in Texas. In a letter to his cousin he wrote, "Texas is the finest portion of the globe that has ever crossed my vision."

In 1835 he bought four thousand acres of land and opened a law office in Nacogdoches. It was not long before colonists came to him for advice. They wanted Sam to lead men to fight against Santa Anna, the Mexican president who had said he would drive all Texans back to the United States. However, Sam met with fifty-eight colonists at Washington-on-the-Brazos. On March 2, 1836, they all signed a Declaration of Independence from Mexico. Sam agreed to be commander-in-chief for the Texans and went about gathering men for an army.

Meanwhile, Santa Anna marched five thousand soldiers against the Alamo, which was being held by Texans in San Antonio. After thirteen days of fighting, all of the 187 Texans were lost.

When hundreds more Texans were killed at Goliad, General Houston knew his small army could not yet stand against thousands of Mexican soldiers. For six weeks he hurried his men through East Texas, leading the Mexicans farther away from their base of supplies.

At last on April 21, 1836, the Texans trapped the Mexicans at San Jacinto. Shouting "Remember the Alamo" and "Remember Goliad," they surprised the Mexicans during siesta time. In eighteen minutes the Texans won the battle.

16

Santa Anna was captured and forced to sign a paper that gave Texas its freedom from Mexico.

While recovering from wounds received in battle, Sam was elected first president of the Republic of Texas. President Houston knew that the new republic was weak and could not hold out by itself. He wrote to President Jackson and asked that Texas be admitted to the United States. The United States legislators said they would not admit Texas because it was a slave-holding state.

After marrying Margaret Lea of Alabama in 1840, Sam became a devoted family man. Although he lived in several different towns, his favorite home was in Huntsville. His farm home near the coast was called Raven Hill in honor of his Indian name.

In 1846, the United States voted to let Texas become the twenty-eighth state. Sam was elected senator and served for ten years in the U.S. Senate. While listening in the Senate, Sam wore his Indian blanket and did a lot of whittling. He carved dozens of pine canes for his friends, and toys for his eight children.

In 1856, Sam was elected governor of Texas. He took his lively family to live in the governor's mansion at Austin.

While he was working to make Texas stronger, a war broke out between the southern and northern states. In February 1861, Texas voted to fight on the side of the South. This was against Sam's wishes. He knew Texas would be hurt by the war.

In great distress, Sam Houston walked the floor all night long in the governor's mansion on the hill. To his wife he said, "Margaret, what shall I do? Turn against my country, or my state?"

With a heavy heart, Sam resigned as governor. He could not agree to let the state of Texas separate itself from the Union. Sam took his family home to Huntsville. There he became ill and died on July 26, 1863.

Not many people heard of Sam's death because newspapers had only enough paper to print the war news. After the war, however, they began to hear and read about the things Sam Houston had done in spite of troubles, failures, and painful wounds. They wrote books and articles about his life. They gathered important papers and furnishings from the Houston family and put them into museums. They named forts, schools, parks, and universities after Sam Houston.

In all these ways they have tried to honor the man who did so much to make Texas strong and free.

Robert Emmett Baylor

1793-1873

Civilizer on Horseback

Before Robert Baylor was born, his parents moved from Virginia to Kentucky. They built a sturdy brick house and a large mill where corn and wheat were ground into flour. When new settlers came to make homes nearby, they called the little community Baylor's Mill.

In 1793, Robert was born at Baylor's Mill. He grew up hearing stories of his father's service as a soldier with George Washington during the revolutionary war. He also heard that his grandfather had been put into prison for preaching with too much zeal about the Baptist religion. Another ancestor had started a college in Oxford, England. And Robert's uncle was a senator from Kentucky.

With a soldier, preacher, lawmaker, and educator in his background, young Robert often wondered if he would choose one of these careers when he grew up. As it turned out, he chose all four of them.

When the Baylors moved to Bourbon County in 1804, Robert was sent to school. Although he did well in his studies, he thought he would like to be a soldier. When he was nineteen, Robert had his wish. He joined the army and went off to fight the British in the War of 1812.

When the war was over, Robert returned to Kentucky to study law. After passing the bar examination, he went into law practice with two of his brothers. In 1819 he was elected to the Kentucky House of Representatives.

By 1821 Robert had moved to Alabama. The people elected him to the Alabama House of Representatives in 1824. Four years later they elected him to Congress during Andrew Jackson's term as president.

When Robert returned to his law practice in Alabama, Creek Indians were attacking white settlers in frequent raids. Robert led a group of men to fight the Indians in 1836. These battles helped bring an end to troubles with the Indians.

So far Robert had been a soldier, lawyer, and lawmaker. It did not seem likely that he would become a preacher too. But one evening in 1838, he went to hear his cousin preach in a church at Talladega. To his astonishment, Robert became a firm believer in Christianity. He joined the Baptist church and was accepted as a minister in 1839.

By now Robert had heard about the newly founded Republic of Texas. Ever since its victory over Mexico, the republic had been struggling to be an independent country.

"Texas needs help," Robert observed. "It has no schools, no law courts, and no churches to speak of."

At age forty-seven, Robert packed up his law books, a Bible, and his beloved violin. He went to Texas and made his home at La Grange in Fayette County. The saddlebags had not been unpacked for long before he became a soldier again. All along the Guadalupe River, Comanche Indians were stealing horses, killing settlers, and burning towns. Robert went as a volunteer with General Burleson to drive away the Indians. He fought in the Battle of Plum Creek near Lockhart in August 1840. After being defeated at Plum Creek, the Indians scattered and moved west.

In La Grange, Robert found time to carry out plans for building a Baptist church and school. He made sure that the school was free to students who could not afford to pay for it. He also organized Texas Baptists into an association and became their first president.

Texans soon found out that Robert was an honest, capable man. In 1841 the Texas Congress chose Robert to be a district judge and a member of the Texas Supreme Court. Into his saddlebags again went the law books, the Bible, the compass, and the Baptist "Covenant of Faith." For the next twenty-three years, Judge Baylor traveled on horseback over five counties in Texas. In many communities he set up courts, schools, and churches.

As interest in education grew, Robert started the Texas Baptist Educational Society. At Washington-on-the-Brazos in March 1845, Judge Baylor and his friends received from the Republic of Texas a charter giving them permission to start a Baptist college. Members of the board voted to name the school after Judge Baylor.

Near the town of Independence, land was donated for the Baylor campus. On the rolling hills, classrooms and dormitories were later built of stone gathered from the countryside. Enrollment grew, but it was a struggle to survive during the Civil War and other troubling times.

Moving closer to the school, Judge Baylor bought a farm

in Washington County. Several times a week, he rode his horse to Independence to teach law classes, which were first offered in 1849. For twenty-four years he taught without pay. During many of those years he also traveled over the state to hold court on weekdays. At night and on Sundays he preached and played his violin at church services wherever he was.

By the end of his long life, Judge Baylor had seen many changes take place in Texas. Indian troubles were almost at an end. Laws had been made for the needs and safety of the state. Court systems, churches, and schools were firmly established. It must have been a great joy to Judge Baylor to know that he helped open so many doors for the people of Texas.

AFTERWORDS

Baylor University joined Waco University in 1886. The name of Baylor was kept for the new school, which opened its campus in Waco in 1887. The Women's Division at Independence was moved to Belton in 1865, where it was known as Baylor Belton. In 1934, it was renamed Mary Hardin-Baylor College.

William Goyens
1794-1856

Determined Citizen of the Texas Frontier

Even though William Goyens was not a slave, it was hard for a black man to live well in North Carolina.

"I'll go to Texas," said William Goyens. "Only a few white people and Indians live there. I'll have a better chance to live as a free man in Texas."

William Goyens arrived in the town of Nacogdoches in 1820. He was twenty-six years old. Like many men of that time, he had never been to school. He could not read. He could write only his name. But William was eager to work.

In 1821, Texas belonged to Mexico. White families came from the United States to make homes and farms on land given to them by Mexico.

"New settlers need nails and tools to build their houses," said William. "Everyone will need wagons. Their horses will need shoes." He decided to become a blacksmith.

William Goyens chose the right line of work. In a short time, his blacksmith shop had so much business that he had to hire men to help him. He built several wagons for himself, and with them he started a business hauling freight between Nacogdoches and Natchitoches, Louisiana.

Many Indian tribes came in from the wilderness to trade

in these towns. William became a friend to the Texas Indians. He understood their ways and learned to speak their languages.

The Mexican government asked William to be its agent to work with the Indians. After making peace treaties with William, the Indians did not bother the settlers around Nacogdoches.

But William had trouble with a few white men. Once while he was traveling in Louisiana in 1826, he was taken captive by a white man. The man wanted to sell William on the slave market.

"I'm not a slave," William protested. "My father was a free man under the law and so am I. You must let me go."

William was not given his freedom until friends came to his rescue. More than ever, William saw how important it was to know his country's laws. He wanted to be sure these laws were obeyed so that all people would be treated fairly. From that time on, he learned as much as he could about the laws of Mexico and the United States.

When people found out how much William knew, they asked him to give legal advice in the courts. They listened to him because they knew he was fair.

By 1836, Texans were struggling to be free from rule by Mexico. General Sam Houston was leader of the Texas army. He did not want the Indians to side with Mexico or to attack the settlers.

General Houston asked William Goyens to meet with Comanche and Cherokee tribes in East Texas. Once again the Indians promised not to make war with the white set-

tlers. This helped the Texans in winning the war against Mexico.

William became more prosperous, and he opened an inn. Nacogdoches was growing quickly as more and more families from the United States came to settle in Texas. The Goyens Inn was a welcome stopping place.

William also bought much land during his lifetime. After a while, he sold some of his land and became wealthy. Some of his white neighbors were envious. They tried to take away his properties. They even tried to make William leave Texas because he was black.

To protect his freedom and his right to own land, William hired lawyers. They took his cases to court and won most of them. William was able to keep his land and his freedom.

On his farm four miles from Nacogdoches, William built a fine two-story house. He named it Goyens Hill. He also ran a gristmill and a sawmill on the creek that ran through his land. With his wife, Mary Sibley, he lived there until his death in 1856.

William Goyens found success because he was trusted in business and in public life. He won respect because he tried to make Texas a place where all people could have the same rights and freedom under the law.

Jane Long
1798-1880

"Mother of Texas"

"Do you think General Long will be coming back soon?" asked Kian. "He has been gone for such a long time."

Jane Long wrapped her shawl more tightly around her thin shoulders. She smiled at the young slave girl.

"We must be patient, Kian. I'm sure my husband will be back just as soon as possible."

"It's so cold and lonesome in the fort all by ourselves," said Kian, as tears rolled down her face.

The year was 1821. Mrs. Long had only her five-year-old daughter, Ann, and Kian to keep her company inside a small mud fort. Their shelter was a tent on the windy shore of Bolivar Point near Galveston Island. Some months before, they had come to Texas from Louisiana to join Jane's husband at the fort.

Shortly after Jane had arrived, the general went to the town of Goliad. He hoped people there would join him in his plan to free Texas from Spanish rule.

"I'll be back soon," General Long had told Jane. "And I will leave a cannon and forty soldiers here at the fort with you."

"We'll wait for you here," promised Jane.

Many weeks passed. General Long did not come back. The soldiers grew tired of waiting. They left camp after begging Jane to go with them, but she would not leave. Now Jane, Ann, Kian, and their dog, Galveston, were alone at the fort.

For more than a year, they stayed at the camp. Each day they gathered wild plants along the shore for food. They caught fish and preserved them in a barrel of salty sea water. Sometimes Jane shot birds for Kian to cook over an open fire. But many times, there was very little to eat.

Jane made a flag from her red petticoat and hung it on a tall pole. She hoped that ships and travelers passing by would see it and stop to bring news of her husband.

Three times, curious Indians paddled their dugout canoes from Galveston Island toward Jane's camp. Each time, Jane and Kian saw them coming. They fired the cannon and the Indians hurried away.

During the severely cold December of 1821, Kian became ill. She was not able to help when Jane gave birth to another little daughter, Mary James. Somehow Jane managed to take care of Kian and her two little girls during the long winter.

Finally, around Christmastime, seven men stopped at the fort with a letter from General Long. He wrote that he had been captured in October and taken to a prison in Mexico. He hoped to be free soon so that he could return to Texas. This news made Jane more determined than ever to stay at the fort.

After three days, the seven men went away. They left fresh venison and some flour for Jane. Once, a ship crossing the bay saw her red flag. The captain stopped and gave food to the hungry campers. He offered to take them aboard, but Jane would not leave.

In March 1822, a man came rowing his boat along the shore. He said he would carry Jane and her little family to the Austin colony a few miles away. At last Jane agreed to go. With Kian and the children she rode in the boat while Galveston ran after them along the shore.

Near the San Jacinto River, Jane moved into a hut made of logs and palmetto leaves. She fished in the river and had a vegetable garden. Her family had plenty to eat while they waited for General Long to return. But on July 8, 1822, a letter was brought to Jane. It said that her husband had been killed in Mexico City. Now there was no reason for Jane to hope any longer.

Some time later, Jane took the girls to her sister's home in Louisiana. In 1824, she came back to Texas as a member of the Austin colony. In the town of Brazoria, Jane and Kian ran a boarding house for seven years. They did all the laundry and cooking for the guests. When the colonists determined to fight Mexico in 1835, Jane stored guns and gunpowder for them in her hotel.

Sam Houston, Mirabeau Lamar, David Burnet, and other Texas leaders often gathered in Jane's hotel to plan the revolution against Mexico. Once, when Stephen F. Austin made a speech there, Jane saw that he looked rather shabby. In a short while she made a buckskin suit for him.

After Texas became a republic, Jane received a large grant of land two miles from Richmond. With the help of Kian's daughter, she turned her land into a highly successful plantation.

In the town of Richmond, she opened a fine hotel. Prominent people of the republic often stopped there to enjoy Jane's hospitality.

In her last days, Jane sat in a rocking chair on her front porch, smoking her pipe. She never failed to entertain visitors with her constant good humor. With her grandson as company on the plantation, she lived to be eighty-two years old.

Because of her great courage, and because it is believed that she bore the first child of English descent in Texas, Jane Long is known as the "Mother of Texas."

Gail Borden
1801-1874

Publisher, Inventor, and Patriot

Two brothers guided a large raft down the Ohio and Mississippi rivers in the summer of 1821. The raft was loaded with meat, hides, corn, and other products to be sold in New Orleans.

It took three weeks for Tom and Gail Borden to make the river trip from their home in Indiana. Soon after they arrived, they sold everything on the raft. As they talked with people in New Orleans, they learned that Stephen F. Austin was there to find families who would move to Texas. Mr. Austin told them that Mexico, of which Texas was a part, would give many acres of free land to each family.

It did not take long for Tom to decide to join the Austin colony in Texas. But Gail Borden went to Mississippi. For seven years, he taught school in Amite County and also worked as a surveyor.

After his marriage, Gail and his wife, Penelope, moved to Texas. By the next year, 1830, Gail was chief surveyor for the Austin colony. He also worked as a secretary for Mr. Austin in San Felipe.

When Stephen Austin went to Mexico City in 1834, he asked Gail Borden to help manage the colony while he was

34

gone. Gail was kept busy with the problems of the settlers. One of the problems was that Mexico stopped allowing families from the United States to come to Texas. Then the colonists became angry when they heard that Mexican officials had put Stephen Austin in jail in Mexico City.

Gail and Tom Borden decided that the settlers needed news about these events. The Bordens ordered a printing press from New Orleans so that they could publish a newspaper.

In October 1835, the first issue of the *Telegraph and Texas Register* came off the press. It was difficult to find enough paper to print it on each week. But the Bordens managed to have eight-page issues and to put out an issue every Saturday.

In 1836, the *Telegraph* reported news of battles for independence from Mexico. Settlers read about the fall of the Alamo and the killings at Goliad. When they heard that Santa Anna's army was moving toward San Felipe, they hurriedly burned their houses and left.

The Bordens put their printing press on a wagon and carried it to Harrisburg (Houston). Once again, they had to flee from Santa Anna. They left the press behind. Mexican soldiers found the press and threw it into the bay.

A few weeks later, Texas defeated Mexico at the Battle of San Jacinto. Gail bought another printing press. In Columbia, the capital of the new republic, he printed reports of the laws being made by the new government.

When the capital was moved to Houston in May 1837, Gail Borden moved his press there. In a short while, he sold his share of the *Telegraph* in order to take a new job. He was appointed the first collector of customs in the busy port of Galveston. Later he helped develop the city by selling land to people who came there to live.

Much of Gail's spare time was spent in his workshop on inventions. With his brother Tom, he invented a locomotive bathhouse for women who wanted to swim in the Gulf of Mexico. It was not considered proper for women to swim in public. But the bathhouse hid the swimmer in an enclosure which could be moved from the beach into the water. It was popular for a short time.

Another invention of Gail's was called a terraqueous machine. It was a carriage with sails. It moved with the wind, whether on land or on water. The Bordens invited a group of friends to take the first ride. All went well as they sped along the beach. But when the terraqueous machine tipped over, everyone quickly lost enthusiasm for it.

In the 1840s, Gail turned to other kinds of inventions. Becoming interested in ways of processing foods, he mixed dried meat and flour into a biscuit. For seven years he tried to find a market for his product. But the biscuit was not a success. People did not like its flavor.

After moving to New York in 1851, Gail worked on the invention that eventually made him world famous. He discovered a way to put milk into a vacuum in cans. His canned milk did not spoil, even in hot weather. He opened a factory in Connecticut, but people still did not buy the canned milk.

After his business failed twice, Gail bought a horse and

wagon and peddled the milk in New York City. It was a difficult time while he tried to support a family of seven children.

In 1858, while riding a train, Gail met a man who offered him the money to build a new factory in Connecticut. This time Gail's invention met with success. Because of the Civil War, milk for soldiers was in great demand. The business grew so fast that Gail opened four more factories. He also developed processes for condensing fruit juices and for making extracts from beef and coffee.

After the Civil War, Texas became a part of the United States again and grew rapidly. Gail went back to Texas to build a meatpacking plant at Borden, the town named for him. He also ran a sawmill and barrel factory at Bastrop.

Gail Borden began using his fortune to help people who were in need. Because black and white children attended separate schools then, he built schools for both of them. He also started Sunday schools for black families, built five churches, and helped pay salaries for numerous missionaries, ministers, students, and teachers.

In a letter he wrote once to Stephen Austin, Gail Borden said, "My maxim is to do the best for my country, praise or no praise."

Ferdinand Lindheimer

1801-1879

Pioneering Texas Naturalist

Times were hard in Germany. The king was forcing the German people to pay for wars they did not want to fight. If they protested, he put them in jail.

One of the protestors was Ferdinand Lindheimer, a young professor. He loudly disagreed with the king's orders. When Ferdinand learned that he would be arrested, he gathered his belongings and left Germany. He caught a sailing ship to America in 1833.

After visiting German friends in Illinois, Ferdinand went to Mexico. With his knowledge of plants, he had no trouble finding work. For sixteen months he managed banana and pineapple plantations in Mexico. In his spare time he collected insects and plants in order to study them.

Texas's political troubles were of great interest to Ferdinand too. When Mexican general Santa Anna took soldiers to Texas to force settlers to obey him, Ferdinand hurried to the coast. He boarded a ship crossing the Gulf of Mexico to the north. It was his plan to join the Texas army to fight Santa Anna and the Mexican soldiers.

As the ship neared the coast of Alabama, it was wrecked. Ferdinand had to swim ashore. Quickly as he could, he made his way to Texas. However, he arrived the day after the Texans' victory at San Jacinto. Sam Houston and his army had captured Santa Anna and most of his soldiers. Texas was now a republic, free from rule by Mexico.

Ferdinand decided to make his home in the new republic. While farming near Houston, he took pride in finding plants that no one else had studied. He knew that only one other man had tried to classify varieties of plants in Texas. Still, how could he make a living by exploring the land for plants?

Fortunately for Ferdinand, Harvard University in Massachusetts was looking for someone to gather and classify plants in the new Republic of Texas. When Ferdinand wrote to Harvard, Dr. Asa Gray was glad to give him the job.

Ferdinand immediately bought a horse, two spotted hunting dogs, and a two-wheeled cart with a canvas over the top. The canvas protected supplies of flour, coffee, salt, and large packets of silk tissues to be used for pressing flower specimens.

With his dogs, horse, gun, and cart, Ferdinand walked all over Galveston Island, Houston, and the East Texas counties of Waller, Washington, Austin, and Colorado. Most of the specimens he gathered were wildflowers. After carefully removing a plant from the ground, Ferdinand dried it between sheets of silk tissue. Then the plant was pressed between heavy boards. Ferdinand preserved thousands of specimens this way. Throughout the next ten years, he sent them to Dr. Gray at Harvard. He also sold thousands more to museums in America and Europe.

In December 1844, Ferdinand had a different job to perform. He was hired as a guide for a group of colonists arriving from Germany. Their leader, Prince Solms-Braunfels, had bought land for the colonists on the Comal and Guadalupe rivers in central Texas. When he learned that Ferdinand Lindheimer knew how to talk with the Indians and knew how to find his way through the wilderness, Prince Solms asked him to lead the colonists to their land.

Ferdinand met the German settlers at the coast and led the way west. It was a long, dangerous trip. Ox carts carried the baggage but the colonists had to walk. There was much sickness and many people died along the way. More than forty children were left as orphans. But Ferdinand brought the survivors to the banks of the Comal in March 1835. They wasted no time in building cabins and planting gardens.

For his work as a guide, Ferdinand received a grant of land in the town of New Braunfels. It was on the banks of the Comal, and had space for a large garden. After building a log cabin, Ferdinand went out into the wilderness to search for wildflowers. Often he was gone for months at a time. Indians watched him secretly as he dug roots and gathered leaves and flowers. They thought he must be looking for plants to use as medicines. For this reason they left him alone.

After marrying Eleanor Reinarz in 1848, Ferdinand built a larger cabin. In one room he put a printing press. Setting his own type in German, he published the town's first newspaper, the *Neu Braunfelser Zeitung,* in 1852. Ferdinand wanted the townspeople to understand clearly what it meant to be a part of Texas and the United States.

For twenty years, Ferdinand published the newspaper to "defend Truth and Right," as he put it. Once his readers were angered by an article he wrote. They threw his printing press into the Comal River. But Ferdinand fished it out and went right on printing.

During the Civil War, it was difficult to find paper for printing. Ferdinand thought it was important for people to receive news. He printed the war news on the silk tissues that he had carefully saved for pressing plants.

While publishing the *Zeitung*, Ferdinand no longer collected plants for museums. However, he never stopped his search for wildflowers around New Braunfels. Today his plant specimens are in the Smithsonian Institution, the St. Louis Botanical Gardens, and in museums in Milwaukee, Paris, Geneva, Madrid, and London.

Botanists recognized the importance of Ferdinand Lindheimer's work as a naturalist. They gave his name to thirty-two of the plants he had discovered. Today his name is part of the scientific Latin name for each of these flowers.

Because of his pioneering work with plants, Ferdinand Lindheimer is called the "Father of Texas Botany."

William Barret Travis

1809-1836

Hero of the Alamo

Nine-year-old William Travis stood in the back of a large covered wagon as it rattled over a dusty road in South Carolina. Waving his cap high above his head, he shouted to a small figure in the distant haze.

"Goodbye, Jim! Don't forget me. I'll see you again!"

Young William was leaving his friend, Jim Bonham, as the Travis family moved to Alabama. Living on neighboring plantations, the two boys had become close friends. Together they rode their ponies to the log schoolhouse each weekday in winter. Carefree summer days were spent fishing, hunting, and looking for adventures in the woods.

Then William's father sold his plantation. He moved his large family, slaves, wagons, and tools to a farm near Sparta, Alabama. When the farm prospered, William went to the Sparta Academy. High-spirited William delighted in playing pranks on his teachers and schoolmates.

A friend, Judge James Dellett, watched with interest as William became a good scholar and a graduate of the academy. He offered to tutor William in the study of law. William eagerly began law studies while teaching school to make a living.

By now William was six feet tall, with keen blue eyes, red hair, and a confident manner. His usual attire included red pantaloons, a white hat, and shiny black boots. With his handsome appearance and liking for fun, William gained friends quickly wherever he went.

At nineteen, William finished his studies and began a successful law practice in the neighboring towns of Claiborne and Clarksville. A year later, he married Rosanna Cato, the daughter of a wealthy planter. A son was born to them in 1829, and in the same year William became an officer in the Alabama militia. But William was deeply unhappy because of his faltering marriage.

Around this time he read a newspaper story that caught his interest. It reported that in Texas, which was a part of Mexico, a family could have 4,428 acres of land for a thirty-dollar fee. A settler need only to promise loyalty to Mexico and to become a member of the Catholic church.

Overnight William made the decision to go to Texas. Taking his slave, Joe, he left Alabama early in 1831. On horseback they swam the Alabama River to join a wagon train. Going by way of New Orleans and Nacogdoches, they arrived in the port of Anahuac on March 2, 1831.

William quickly learned to speak Spanish and began the study of Mexican law. He intended to be a good lawyer and Mexican citizen. It was not long, however, before he clashed with the authorities. With his new law partner, Patrick Jack, he refused to pay taxes demanded by the Mexicans. Both men were put in prison by the military commander at Anahuac.

Within several weeks, furious Texans marched to the prison, captured the guards, and freed the two men from jail. William and Patrick decided to move where life would be safer: San Felipe de Austin, Stephen F. Austin's colony of Americans.

In San Felipe there were only thirty log houses. But there were also shops, hotels, taverns, a printing plant, hospital, and even a billiard hall. There was also a clothing store where William could shop to his heart's content. One of the first things he ordered was a wide-brimmed white wool hat that was guaranteed to be waterproof. With his fine clothes, many new friends, and Patrick Jack as his partner, William settled down to a flourishing law practice.

His temper flared again, however, when Mexican president Santa Anna sent soldiers to force settlers to pay more taxes and to give up their guns. The Texans were already angry because Stephen Austin had been kept in a Mexico City prison for more than a year.

"The time has come to defend our rights," declared William at a meeting in San Felipe. With twenty men, he marched to Anahuac in June 1835. He demanded the surrender of the commander of the fort and made him leave town. When Santa Anna heard about this, he ordered the arrest of William and all the men who sided with him. But the colonists protected them from being captured.

Stephen Austin was allowed to return to Texas in July. However, the colonists knew it was no longer possible to keep peace with Mexico. William rode to towns in Texas to find men to join an army. He also wrote to his childhood friend

Jim Bonham asking him to come help Texas fight for its freedom.

Sam Houston was chosen to lead an army against Mexico. General Houston ordered James Bowie to go with his soldiers to the town of Béxar (San Antonio). He told him to destroy the buildings of the Alamo garrison so that Mexican soldiers could not make use of them.

At about the same time, Texas governor Henry Smith ordered William Travis to defend Béxar with a small cavalry troop. Using his own money to buy food and blankets for the men, William reached the Alamo on February 3, 1836. There to greet him was his faithful friend Jim Bonham who had joined James Bowie and his volunteers.

The Texans knew that a large Mexican army was coming to capture Béxar. They decided to stay in the Alamo to defend it. After several arguments about who was in charge, James Bowie and William Travis agreed to share the command. Working as hard and fast as their men, they dug wells and mended walls. Corn, cattle, and guns were brought into the garrison.

Scouts reported that Santa Anna was coming with more than twelve hundred soldiers. William knew that the Texans would have difficulty defending the Alamo. Twice he sent Jim Bonham with letters to the towns of Goliad and Gonzales. The letters were requests for soldiers and supplies, and ended with the words "Victory or Death." But each time Bonham returned with sad news. No one was coming to help.

James Bowie became seriously ill, and William took command. Time was running short. The Mexican army had been sighted close to town. William made sure that cannon were placed on the walls and that each man had ammunition. He knew that 187 Texans could not win against an army that now included five thousand men. He gave his men a choice. They could choose to leave the Alamo and get to safety, he told them, or they could stay and fight. Only one man left. All others, including Jim Bonham, said they would fight to the death.

On February 23 the Mexicans surrounded the Alamo. From high on the walls, the Texans aimed rifles and cannon with accuracy into masses of soldiers. The Mexicans could not get close. Thirteen days passed before the Mexicans threw ladders up and climbed the walls to get into the Alamo grounds. Then, greatly outnumbered, every Texan was lost in the fierce hand-to-hand fighting. The end of the battle came the morning of March 6, 1836.

William Travis had lived only twenty-six years. Yet his courage and that of his men greatly inspired the Texas army. Six weeks later at the Battle of San Jacinto, the Texans defeated Santa Anna and his men. Freedom was won.

To Texas and to all people of the world, William Travis and the Alamo became a symbol of bravery and steadfastness that would never be forgotten.

John O. Meusebach
1812-1897

"Texas Forever"

A tall, red-bearded man stood at the railing of a ship. Its great white sails billowed high above his head. Shading his eyes with his hand, he looked towards the shoreline of Texas.

"There it is at last," said John Meusebach. "This is the land where our German colonists can live as free people. We shall never have to bow down to a king again."

When the ship landed in Galveston, John immediately bought a horse. He was in a hurry to get to a tiny settlement in the wilderness of central Texas. There, on the banks of the Comal River, German settlers were building cabins. Under the guidance of their leader, Prince Solms, they had named their village New Braunfels.

It was May 1845. Prince Solms wanted to go back to Germany. John Meusebach, agreeing to take his place, had come from Germany to manage the colony. He hoped to learn from the prince of the many things that needed to be done. When John reached New Braunfels, however, Prince Solms was not there. He had gone to Galveston to catch a ship back to Germany.

John rode to Galveston. When he arrived, he found the prince being held by a group of angry men.

"He hasn't paid us for wagons, tools, oxen, or food for his colony," they said. "We won't let him go until he pays us what he owes."

In order for Prince Solms to be able to return home, John paid the huge debts. This meant he had nothing left. And very soon a great deal more money would be needed, because hundreds more German colonists were coming once again.

This was only the beginning of troubles for John Meusebach. But he felt sure that the Verein, a society of twenty wealthy noblemen in Germany, would send money when they heard how badly it was needed. The Verein had promised to support German families who wanted to go to the Republic of Texas. In fact, the Verein was also known as the Society for the Protection of German Immigrants in Texas.

Although the Verein sent a little money from time to time, it was never enough. The German settlers became angry. They blamed John Meusebach. John said nothing, however, and only worked harder to get the colony started. He wanted to keep the promises made to the settlers.

Because he had been trained in law and finance at German universities, John was a good businessman. He set up a bookkeeping system to keep track of expenses in the colony. He borrowed money to build houses and to buy seeds, carts, horses, oxen, plows, food, and other supplies. It helped John to remember his family's motto: *"Tenax Propositi."* These Latin words mean "Persevere in What You Undertake." John Meusebach was determined to persevere.

The Germans had bought almost four million acres of land in central Texas without seeing it. No one had told them that thousands of Indians roamed over the land. When John found this out, he knew that peace would have to be made with the Indians before the land could be opened up to white farmers.

John paid a visit to the small Waco tribe that was camped on the Comal River. The Wacos had never seen red hair. Twenty squaws grabbed John and pulled him into the river. They scrubbed his hair and beard in the clear water. When the reddish-gold color did not change, they laughed and ran off into the woods. Then John and the chief smoked the pipe of peace and became friends.

Once again John heard that the Verein was sending him hundreds of new settlers. Still, they were not sending money or supplies. In desperation, John wrote a letter to a newspaper in Germany. After the letter was published, the German people raised a large amount of money. They sent it by a special messenger to Texas. It reached New Braunfels on September 7, 1846. Now John was able to pay some of the debts.

In order to prepare for more immigrants. John asked surveyors to measure the land that had been bought. The surveyors were afraid. The land John wanted measured was Comanche hunting ground. They refused to enter it unless a peace treaty was made with the Comanches.

To be nearer the Indian Territory, John and 120 settlers built a way station and called it Fredericksburg. Five hundred people were living there by the end of 1846. Over four thousand new German settlers were on their way by then also, though. Where would these people live? John was tired and discouraged, but once again he remembered his family motto, "Persevere in What You Undertake."

With a group of forty men on horseback, three wagons, and several hunters to find food along the way, John set out for the Comanche camps on the San Saba River. Near the Llano River at present-day Mason, Comanche chief Ketemoczy came to meet them. After talking with John through an interpreter, he promised to bring twenty chiefs to the San Saba when the moon was full. They would talk about peace.

While they waited for the full moon, John and several men explored the land near the river. They studied the rocks, soil, and plants so that they would know how the land could be used by the settlers.

On March 2, 1847, the meeting with the Comanches was held. Several hundred warriors on horseback lined up on one side while squaws and children lined up on the other. The chiefs sat on buffalo robes in the center.

John and seventeen men rode in front of each line of Indians. They shot their guns into the air until they were empty. This was to show the Indians that they had come as friends. The Indians admired their bravery. They gave a special name to John, calling him *El Sol Colorado* (The Red Sun). They said they looked up to him as they looked up to the sun.

John and his men sat on a buffalo robe in the circle with the chiefs. For two days they talked and smoked the peace pipe. The Indians agreed to allow white families to settle in their territory. The white men promised the Indians three thousand dollars in presents and told the Indians they would be welcome to trade in their towns. The treaty was a success. It was never broken by either the white men or the Indians.

While John was working for the colonists, Texas had become part of the United States. After John resigned from the Verein, he was elected to the state senate in 1850. He also became land commissioner for the colonists. At last he was able to make certain that the settlers received the land promised to them by the Verein.

In 1852, John married Agnes Coreth. In New Braunfels, Fredericksburg, and on a farm at Waco Springs, they raised seven children. The Meusebachs made their last home on a seven-hundred-acre farm between Mason and Fredericksburg. John opened a store and post office for the community, which he called Loyal Valley. Here he delighted in greeting friends and in growing great varieties of fruits, vegetables, and flowers.

At his death at the age of eighty-five, John Meusebach was buried near his farm in a family cemetery. On his tombstone were chiseled two lines that were his life's mottoes. One was *Tenax Propositi*. The other was *Texas Forever*.

Cynthia Ann Parker

1827-1864

Young Captive of the Comanches

The morning was quiet at Fort Parker on May 19, 1836. Most of the men had gone to work in the fields nearby. Children played by the log cabins inside the fort. Their mothers were busy cooking the noon meal.

Suddenly, the quiet of the day was broken. A large band of Indians on horseback rode up to the gate.

Nine-year-old Cynthia Ann Parker ran to hold tightly to her mother's hand. She watched as her Uncle Ben walked to the gate. She saw him shake his head and knew he was telling the Indians that he had no beef to give them.

The Indians were angry. They shouted loud war whoops. Kicking their horses, they rode wildly into the fort. They shot arrows in every direction.

Women and children ran in terror from the cabins. A few of them were able to escape. They hid in the woods by a spring near the fort. But some of the white people were killed.

Cynthia Ann and her brother John were snatched up by yelling Comanches and tied to a horse. Then the Indians left so quickly that no one could follow them.

For days, Cynthia Ann and John rode with the Indians.

56

They rode far from their home in East Texas. Soon Cynthia Ann was separated from her brother and taken to a Comanche camp. She was lonely and frightened. Indian words were strange to her, and she did not understand the Indian ways.

But after many months, Cynthia Ann was not lonely anymore. She forgot the English language. She learned to live and talk as an Indian. The Comanches called her Naduah. They taught her to sew buffalo hides for tepees and moccasins. She learned to chew tough deerskins to soften them for dresses and shirts. She picked berries to mix with buffalo meat and bear grease. This made a sausage called pemmican.

When she dyed her skin with berry juices, she even looked like an Indian. There were only three things Cynthia Ann could not change. These were her blue eyes, brown hair, and the freckles on her face.

Twenty-four years passed. Texas joined the United States, and thousands of white settlers came to Texas. The Indians did not want white people settling on their hunting grounds, and they fought the settlers. But they gradually lost both the battles and their land.

On December 18, 1860, Captain Sul Ross led a group of Texas Rangers to attack a band of Indians on the Pease River. Only a few warriors escaped. The rest were killed.

After the battle, a lone Indian came to look at the fallen warriors. One of the rangers raised his rifle to shoot. The Indian lifted her arms high. She held a baby to show she was not a warrior.

The rangers walked closer to her. They saw that she had blue eyes, brown hair, and freckles on her face. They could tell then that she was a white woman.

The woman did not want to leave the battleground. The rangers put her and her baby on a horse. They took them to Fort Cooper, and then sent for Isaac Parker. They knew that Isaac had searched for his niece ever since her capture at Fort Parker years ago.

The blue-eyed woman would not look at Isaac Parker. When he spoke she would not answer. She only sat still, holding the baby. Then Isaac said, "The name of my brother's child was Cynthia Ann."

The woman looked up. These were the first words she had understood. She said, "Me Cincy Ann. Me Cincy Ann."

Isaac Parker was overjoyed. He found a man who could speak the Comanche language. He asked Ben Kiggins to talk to Cynthia Ann alone.

Ben spoke with Cynthia Ann. She told him she was the wife of Chief Peta Nocona. Their two sons had disappeared in the battle with the rangers. She had been looking for them on the battleground when the rangers had found her.

Cynthia Ann told Ben Kiggins she remembered that her parents were white people. With a stick, she drew a picture of Fort Parker on the ground. She filled her mouth with water from a canteen. Then she dripped it on the place where a river had run by the fort. After this, Ben and Isaac were sure that she was Cynthia Ann Parker.

Isaac Parker took Cynthia Ann and her baby, Prairie Flower, to homes of relatives. Everyone tried to make her feel welcome. They combed her hair and gave her new clothes to wear.

But Cynthia Ann was not happy among these people. She would not wear the new clothes. She would not speak to her relatives. Several times she tried to run away. She wanted to find her sons. She longed to go back to the plains where she had lived as an Indian.

Little Prairie Flower died of a fever when she was only two years old. Cynthia Ann was so unhappy that she would not eat. She became so ill that nothing could save her.

Cynthia Ann died at the home of her white relatives. One of her sons later became the greatest of all Comanche chiefs in Texas. He called himself Quanah Parker.

But that is another story.

Elisabet Ney
1833-1907

Artist Against All Odds

Elisabet stamped her foot and shouted.

"I *will* go to art school. No one can stop me."

Mrs. Ney looked at her daughter in astonishment.

"It's impossible, Elisabet. Girls are not allowed in art classes here in Germany."

"And besides," said Mr. Ney, "you are seventeen years old. Soon you will marry. An education would be a waste of time."

Elisabet shook her head. "I will be a sculptor. My mind is made up."

To her parents' dismay, Elisabet did become a sculptor. She was the first woman allowed to enter classes at the art academy in Munich, Germany. There she graduated at the top of her class and was given a scholarship to study in Berlin.

It was not long before everyone in Germany had heard about the remarkable young Miss Ney. She traveled all over Europe. Her works were entered in competitions. King George V and King Wilhelm of Prussia asked her to make statues of them.

In 1865 Elisabet married Edmund Montgomery, a doctor. But she would not let Edmund tell anyone they were married. She wanted to be sure that everyone would still call her Miss Ney. Even Edmund called her Miss Ney.

Elisabet and her husband wanted to get away from the wars being fought in Europe. In 1870 they came to the United States. After two years in Georgia, they moved to Hempstead, Texas. There they bought a large cotton plantation, Liendo.

Elisabet ran Liendo while her husband practiced medicine and wrote scientific articles. She directed the workers in planting and harvesting crops. There was no time for her sculpture, especially after two sons were born to the Montgomerys.

The women in Hempstead found Elisabet strange because she was so different from them. They wore their hair and their skirts very long. Elisabet cut her curly red hair short and wore loose gowns over purple woolen bloomers. And when her neighbors came to call, Elisabet served them buttermilk and dry toast instead of tea and cake.

Few people in Texas knew that Miss Ney had been a sculptor in Europe. The governor of Texas, Oran Roberts, knew of her though. In 1883 he asked Elisabet to give advice on the design of the new capitol that was being built in Austin.

At about the same time, Elisabet was asked to make statues of Sam Houston and Stephen F. Austin for the World's Fair to be held in Chicago. Elisabet was fifty-nine years old and had done very little work as a sculptor for twenty years, but that did not stop her. She moved to Austin and set up a workshop in the basement of the capitol.

Elisabet had not forgotten the steps to take for making a piece of sculpture. After drawing the subject, she formed a small doll-size model with clay. When she was satisfied with it, she then made a heavy wire support of the height she wished the finished statue to be. Around the wire, called an armature, she molded moist clay into the shape of a figure. At the outer edges she placed thin metal pieces called shims. The clay model was then coated with wet plaster and left to harden.

The dried mold was pried apart at the seam made by the shims, leaving the two halves bearing the imprint of the figure. After the two halves were glued together with wet plaster, the hollow mold was filled with more wet plaster. When it was completely dry, the mold was chipped away to reveal the finished plaster figure.

Like other sculptors of the time, Elisabet wanted the final figure to be of marble because it was a stone that would never crumble. It would last forever, while plaster cracked easily. Since the finest marble was found in Europe, she sometimes took her plaster figures to Italy where marble was quarried. There the stonecutters made exact measurements of each figure and cut the marble to match. After bringing the marble figure back to Texas, Elisabet would add final details with special cutting tools, chisels, and hammers.

It took a long time to complete a statue. Elisabet was able to finish only the figure of Sam Houston for the Chicago fair. Texans were proud when the statue turned out to be one of the fair's most popular exhibits. They asked Miss Ney to make more statues of Texas heroes for the Austin capitol and for the nation's capitol in Washington, D.C. Soon Elisabet had so many orders for her work that she built a large studio in Austin and made it her home.

In her studio, Elisabet spent the next fifteen years doing some of the best work of her life. Her last piece, a statue of Lady Macbeth, is now in the Smithsonian Institution in Washington, D.C. Other works are in museums and castles in Europe, at the University of Texas, in cemeteries, and in her Austin home.

Miss Ney's studio-home is now a museum filled with many of her sculptures and personal belongings. Streams of visitors go each year to see the works of the young woman who once said, "I *will* be a sculptor."

Charles Goodnight

1836-1929

Cattleman

A nine-year-old boy rode a white-faced mare alongside of a covered wagon. With his family, young Charles Goodnight was on the way to Texas. For eight hundred miles he rode bareback, from a farm in southern Illinois to the Brazos River.

Charles and his family were among the first settlers to farm Milam County in 1845. Great herds of buffalo still swarmed over the unfenced land. Indians hunted the huge shaggy animals, following closely behind the herds.

With his keen eyes and ears, Charles Goodnight soon learned the ways of Indians and buffalo. But something else caught his interest even more: longhorn cattle, living wild in the thickets. These wiry, tough creatures held Charles's attention for the rest of his life.

By the time he was twelve, Charles was not only an all-around cowboy, but a student of nature too. While working on a neighbor's ranch, he noticed the way cattle followed a lead bull, and saw how a crash of thunder could frighten them into a stampede. He studied plants and shrubs on the prairie, and knew which ones grew close to water. He knew, as the Indians did, that trails left by animals led to water.

66

He could even tell the freshness of a hoofprint by counting the insect tracks in it. The land and animals of Texas were like school for Charles, and he was eager to learn. He dreamed of being a cattleman, and of having his own ranch someday.

At twenty, Charles had his first chance to own cattle. With his stepbrother, Wes Sheek, he took care of 450 cows for a neighbor. For pay, Charles and Wes received "every fourth calf born and every sixth dollar for each cow sold" from Mr. Claiborn Varner.

In four years, Charles and Wes owned 180 head of cattle. They moved the herd into Keechi Valley in Palo Pinto County. The grass was plentiful there, but so were Comanche and Kiowa Indians. Helped by neighbors, Charles fought the Indians and managed to keep most of his cows and horses from harm.

When a few more families moved in, Charles persuaded his mother and her husband, Adam Sheek, to move to Keechi Valley. They built a log home, which also served as the post office. A room was kept for the schoolteacher who came to the community. One of the teachers was Molly Dyer, a young woman from Tennessee. Charles went to visit his mother more often after he met Molly Dyer. However, many disturbing events took place before their marriage in 1871.

In 1861, most of the soldiers and cowboys left Texas to fight in the Civil War. Charles and a few ranchers were the only ones left to protect the settlers and their homes from Indians. When rangers were sent to help, Charles became a Texas Ranger under Captain Sul Ross. With Ross, he took part in the Pease River battle, where Cynthia Ann Parker was captured with the Comanches.

In 1864 Charles formed a partnership with his new friend, Oliver Loving. With eighteen cowboys, they made their first cattle drive in June 1866. They drove two thousand cattle from Fort Belknap to Fort Sumner, New Mexico.

Returning to Texas, Charles packed the payment of twelve thousand dollars in gold, slabs of bacon, water, and tobacco on a pack mule. One night during a terrible storm on the plains, the pack mule got loose and ran off into the dark. During a wild chase, Charles jumped from his mount and grabbed the pack rope to stop the running mule. The gold was safe, but all the food, water, and tobacco were gone.

For the next few days, Charles and his three companions went hungry and thirsty. "It made me see," Charles later said, "that all our gold could not buy us a drink of water or get us food. From then on, I never worshiped money."

Although Oliver Loving was killed by Indians in 1867, Charles and his cowboys continued to make the drives. For the next three years they made as many as eight drives a year to New Mexico, Wyoming, and Colorado. Each time they drove ten thousand head of cattle. Charles always rode ahead of the herd to scout for water and campsites. Even in strange territory, his sense of direction never failed. "I never carried a compass," he said. "And I never was lost."

The drives were successful and Charles bought several ranches in Colorado. However, in 1876 a Mexican scout told Charles of a long, deep canyon in the flatlands of the Texas Panhandle. "A river runs through it, and the bluffs are so high that it will make a huge natural corral," the scout said.

When he took Charles to see Palo Duro Canyon, Charles knew that the scout was right. A partner in Colorado, John Adair, provided the money to buy the land and more cattle. Calling it the JA Ranch, he built bunkhouses for the cowboys, sheds for tools and equipment, and a main ranch house for Molly and Charles. The management of the herds was left up to Charles. As usual, he was on horseback most of the time, working with the cattle. In a few years the partners had one hundred thousand cattle which they ran on a million acres of land.

When the railroads came to the Panhandle, new towns sprang up. One was named Goodnight. Settlers, called "nesters" by old-timers, came in large numbers to the area. Charles helped them to start farms, churches, schools, law courts, and banks. With his own money, he established Goodnight College and gave it to the Baptist Church.

In 1887 the Goodnights left Palo Duro Canyon and moved to the town of Goodnight. Charles, busy as ever, managed ranches, built fences of newly invented barbed wire, raised herds of buffalo, founded stockmen's associations, and developed new, better breeds of cattle. With his continuing interest in plant life, he planted orchards and scattered wild plum seeds along river banks and in canyons. All the while, he and Molly entertained a constant stream of visitors. One of these was the famed Quanah Parker, who had once brought his tribe of Comanches to hunt buffalo in the Palo Duro Canyon.

Near the end of his long life, Charles lived in Clarendon

during the summers and in Phoenix, Arizona, during the winters. At age ninety-three, with his shock of white hair, his vitality, and his keen interest in the world about him, he attracted people wherever he went. He did not understand why so much attention was given him. Instead he said simply, "It has been my aim in life to try to have the world a little better because I lived in it."

Quanah Parker
1848-1911

Last Great Chief of the Comanches

It was bitterly cold in the winter of 1860. Ice covered the flatlands of the Texas Panhandle. Unable to hunt buffalo, Chief Peta Nocona's tribe of Comanches rested in its camp by the Pease River.

Days passed quietly as the Indian families stayed close by their fires. Squaws left the tepees only to gather wood or to carry water from the river. The men braided ropes of buffalo thongs and fashioned arrows and spears as they waited for warmer weather.

The peaceful days came to an end early one morning. Shouts from the guards brought the Indian families running from their tepees. Grabbing weapons, the men jumped on their horses as the sound of rifles filled the air.

From two directions, the blue-coated Texas Rangers of Captain Sul Ross were attacking the Comanche camp. The Indian warriors fought back as well as they could in the confusion. Many were killed, but Chief Peta Nocona and a few warriors escaped during the battle.

Quanah, the twelve-year-old son of Chief Nocona, ran with his younger brother Pecos to hide in the tall brush by the river. He did not know what was happening to his mother and baby sister. He did know that the Comanches had lost the battle.

"Perhaps the white soldiers will find our mother," Quanah told Pecos. "They will not harm her when they see she is a white woman. But we cannot stay here. I don't want the soldiers to find us and take us too. We don't want to live as white people."

Shivering with cold, Quanah and Pecos walked for many hours to the camp of Chief Horseback, a friend of their father. The chief made Quanah a part of his tribal family. Pecos was sent to another Indian village. He became the adopted son of a couple who had no children. A short time later, however, Quanah heard that Pecos had died from an illness.

During the next six years, Quanah learned to be a warrior. He rode with the Comanches on the Great Plains, from South Texas north to Kansas. With the other Indians, he was determined to keep white families from building homes and towns on the plains. He knew that when white people came, the Indians would not be able to roam the plains to hunt buffalo. Without buffalo hides and meat, the Indians would have no homes, no clothes, and no food.

When he was eighteen, Quanah joined a band of Comanches called the Quahadi. Around his neck he wore a string of eagle claws. His warriors called him "Eagle of the Comanches." They obeyed his orders to burn houses, drive off cattle, and steal horses from the white settlers.

In 1867, Quanah and his braves were asked to meet with white leaders to make peace. At Medicine Lodge in Kansas, they joined with five thousand Indians from other tribes. The white men had brought thirty wagons filled with presents for the Indians. They told the Indians they would be given many acres of land on reservations if they would live as farmers instead of buffalo hunters.

Most of the tribes agreed to move to reservations, but not Quanah. He said, "We do not want to be surrounded by walls. We do not want to live as white men do."

Quanah and his braves went back to the Texas plains. For seven years they searched for buffalo, but the great herds were gone. White hunters had killed millions of the animals and left them to rot in the open. They took only the furs and hides to sell to factories in the eastern United States. Quanah and his people were desperate.

In June 1874, Quanah sent a message to other tribes that were still living on the plains. "Come and talk about making war," it said. Seven hundred warriors in war paint came to join Quanah.

As chief of the war council, he declared, "We will attack the white buffalo hunters in their lodge at Adobe Walls before the sun rises. They are few. We are many."

At the trading post of Adobe Walls in the Panhandle, twenty-eight white hunters were asleep when the Indians hid around their cabin during the night. By chance, a pole holding the roof of the cabin broke. Two men awoke and got up to fix the pole. Near sunrise one of the men, Billy Dixon, went out to find his horse. When he discovered several Indians hiding nearby, he rushed to warn his sleeping friends.

74

For the next three days, a battle raged between the Indians and the hunters. Again and again the Indians charged the lodge. They backed their horses against the heavy log walls, hoping to push them down. The buffalo hunters shot their rifles through cracks between the logs. Many Indians and horses were lost.

Quanah's horse was killed and he was wounded. At last he ordered a retreat. "Arrows are no good against guns," he said.

The next year held only misery for the wandering Indians. Without rain, there were no watering places, grass, or buffalo. Their horses died, their clothes were ragged, and they were starving. All the tribes except the Quahadi moved to reservations.

Then in June 1875, Quanah told his people, "We, too, must travel the white man's road." He led his people to Fort Sill in Oklahoma and surrendered to the white agent. The Comanches were given land on the beautiful grassy Oklahoma plains. But they had to obey the white man's laws. They could no longer roam on the prairies.

The white agent knew that Quanah's mother had been Cynthia Ann Parker. When Cynthia Ann was eight years old, Comanches had taken her from her family. They had raised her, and she had married Chief Peta Nocona. The agent told Quanah that his mother and her baby, Prairie Flower, had been captured at the battle on the Pease River. He also told Quanah that his mother had been sent to live with her white relatives, and that soon after that, she and the baby had died.

With a letter from the agent as an introduction, Quanah went to visit the Parker family. They made him feel welcome. For the first time, Quanah slept on sheets. He ate bread and molasses while sitting at a table. Quanah liked his mother's people so well that he called himself Quanah Parker after that.

"If my mother could learn to accept the ways of Indians, I can learn to accept the ways of white people," he declared.

Going back to his tribe, Quanah spent the rest of his life helping his people to accept new ways. With them, he learned to raise cattle and sheep. He built fences around farms and ranches. He persuaded Comanches to learn English and to obey the white man's laws. He sent his children to school, built a house, and even became part-owner of a railroad. Everywhere in the United States he became known and respected for his work.

The Indians called Quanah their last Great Chief. They saw that he was like a strong bridge between themselves and the white people. His example made it easier for other Indians to "travel the white man's road."

John Avery Lomax

1867-1948

Collector of Cowboy Music and Lore

As soft rain pattered on their cabin roof, the twelve members of the Lomax family slept soundly. From the distance came a low crooning sound through the darkness. It was a cowboy singing and yodeling to his cattle as they plodded up the Chisholm Trail.

Four-year-old John Lomax awoke to hear the peaceful chant. Running to the window, he listened until the cattle had moved beyond the river and he could hear the sound no more.

Living by the Chisholm Trail in the 1870s, young John saw thousands of cattle being driven to northern markets. Drovers let the cows stop at the Bosque River to drink and rest near the Lomax home. While sitting nearby on Selim, his favorite pony, John listened to the singing that seemed to quiet the restless cattle.

O, lay down, dogies,
like you've laid down before,
Lay down, little dogies, lay down.
Whoo-OO-OO-ee-oo-oo.

At an early age, John began to write the words of songs

on pieces of cardboard and scraps of paper. He kept them in a secret place, all rolled up and tied with a piece of cotton string.

Singing was a daily part of pioneer life by the Bosque River. John's parents taught him songs that made the work go faster. As he dropped seed corn into freshly plowed furrows, he chanted:

Whistle and hoe,
Sing as you go;
Shorten the rows
By the songs you know.

Songs with many verses helped him to go on when he grew weary during corn-planting time.

In late summer, John learned hymns at camp meetings held under a brush arbor. Families came in wagons to camp together for a week by the river. All day and into the night, they listened to preaching and sang church songs. There were no hymn books. A song leader sang one line at a time and the people repeated it after him. One of John's favorites was:

I'm bound for the Promised Land,
I'm bound for the Promised Land.
Oh, who will come and go with me?
I'm bound for the Promised Land.

A different kind of singing also captured young John's interest. Negro folk songs and jigs were taught to him by Nat Blythe, a young black man who worked on the Lomax farm. Patting his hands and dancing in jig time, Nat often swung to the lilt of:

Juba dis and Juba dat,
Oh, Juba killed a yaller cat,
Oh, Juba! Juba! Juba!

From visitors who came to the farm and from short sessions of school, John gathered riddles and rhymes. He added them all to his secret roll of folks songs and jingles.

When John was twenty, he planted eleven acres of wheat. His father said that when John sold the wheat, he could use the money for college. With high hopes, John watched the wheat grow tall during the summer. However, the Bosque flooded after heavy rains and the wheat crop lay in ruins. John sifted out the mud as well as he could. The few wheat seeds left were ground into flour. But the flour didn't bring enough money to pay for his college fees. With a heavy heart, John sold his beloved pony, Selim. He never forgot that Selim helped pay for his first year at Granbury College.

In September 1887, John rode in a wagon to enter school in Granbury, Texas. At the bottom of his trunk was the roll of cowboy songs, tied with the piece of cotton string.

After one year at Granbury, John taught school for seven years. In the summers he went to Chautauqua, New York, to study Latin, math, and English. Literature courses led him to further study at the University of Texas.

To his English literature professor, John shyly showed his collection of cowboy songs as an example of American folk literature. The professor, though kind, told John that songs of the frontier were worthless. In great disappointment, John burned the scraps of his songs that night behind his dormitory.

While teaching at Texas A&M University in 1906, John was given a scholarship to graduate school at Harvard University. During a course in American literature, Professor Barrett Wendell asked his students to turn in a thesis.

"Write about the literature in the part of the country where you have lived," Professor Wendell said. When John asked if he could write about cowboy songs of the western frontier, the professor met his idea with enthusiasm.

To collect the songs, John sent a letter to a thousand newspapers. They published his letters, which asked readers to send ballads and songs to John. From every part of the country the ballads poured in — from old buffalo hunters, stage drivers, cowboys, stockmen, saloon keepers, and farmers' wives. In fact, the letters kept coming in for the next twenty years.

Although working as a banker to support a wife and four children, John devoted his life to collecting American folk songs. With help from his son Alan, he traveled thousands of miles down the backroads of America. They were looking for people who could still remember the old songs that no one had ever written down. These songs were in danger of being completely forgotten.

Carrying a clumsy recording machine called a dictaphone, they visited with mountaineers, prisoners, lumbermen, miners, farmhands, sailors, and even gypsies. Most of these people refused to sing into the large horn of the recording machine. So John and Alan wrote down the words and tunes.

From a gypsy came the words and music of "Git Along

Little Dogie" and "Goodbye Old Paint." Other people gave him "Sweet Betsy from Pike," "Home on the Range," and many other songs that soon became popular across the country.

John's first book of collections, *Cowboy Songs and Ballads*, was published in 1910. This was the first time that American folk songs had been printed with both words and music. Four more books followed as interest grew in native songs and spirituals. John and Alan added more than ten thousand songs to the American folk songs listed in the archives of the Library of Congress. Funny, sad, lively, somber — all of them told the story of the plain people of America who had struggled to find a place in the new land.

Because of the careful work of John Lomax and his family, these stories in song have been saved for all of America in the years to come.

Chester Nimitz
1885-1966

Admiral From the Hill Country

Captain Karl Nimitz had built his hotel in the shape of a Mississippi River steamboat. It stood by the broad main street in the tiny village of Fredericksburg, Texas. There was a mast and even a pilot's house, called the "crow's nest," at the very top. The Steamboat Hotel could be seen for miles around. It was a Texas landmark when Karl's grandson Chester first lived in it.

On many afternoons, young Chester Nimitz sat in the crow's nest with his white-bearded Grandfather Karl. From their perch they could see the tidy farmlands that dotted surrounding hills. Below them, ruddy-faced German farmers guided horse teams pulling heavy wagons down wide streets. Wearing sunbonnets, women with baskets on their arms chatted in German as they gathered in small groups by the storefronts.

Across the street, Chester could see the small cottage where he had been born in 1885. Since his father had died before his birth, Chester and his mother had come to live with Grandfather Karl in the Steamboat Hotel.

The hotel was a lively place. Passing through it each week were soldiers, ranchers, salesmen, and travelers from other lands. In the evenings, guests gathered to swap stories with Grandfather Karl. Chester heard about faraway places, as well as tales of Indians and pioneers who lived nearby. He listened intently as his grandfather told favorite sea stories about his service in the German merchant marine. As he ended his stories, Grandfather Karl often said to his guests, "Someday my grandson Chester will be an admiral in the United States Navy. You'll see, it will happen."

Young Chester had never seen the ocean, and he was not at all sure he would like it. It was more to his liking to be in the Texas Hill Country near the warmth of family and friends in the little village.

When his mother remarried and moved to Kerrville, Chester sadly left his grandfather and the Steamboat Hotel. Since it was not far to Fredericksburg, he went back to hunt and fish with his grandfather every summer and at Christmastime. During each visit, Grandather Karl reminded him, "Do your best, Chester, and do not worry about the things over which you have no control." It was advice Chester remembered for the rest of his life.

During high school years, Chester earned room and board by working at a hotel in Kerrville. Although his grades were good and school friends made days pass pleasantly, Chester grew restless with small-town life. He wanted to see the world beyond Texas.

At age fifteen, he met two young army officers who suggested he go to West Point Military Academy. Chester liked the idea. "In the army," he thought, "I'll get to see foreign countries and travel around the world."

When he wrote to his congressman in San Antonio to ask for an appointment to the academy, Congressman Slayton wrote back, "There is no opening at West Point now. But there is a place for a midshipman at Annapolis Naval Academy. Will you take it?"

Although he had never heard of the naval academy, and did not even know where it was, Chester decided to go there. In addition to travel, he wanted a college education. And besides, he knew it would please Grandfather Karl.

When Chester passed the examinations for the naval academy, Grandfather Karl arranged a celebration for all of Fredericksburg. It was the first community "wurstfest," held at the Steamboat Hotel in May 1901. People came from all around to show their pride in Chester's accomplishment.

Graduation was in January 1905 when Chester was not yet twenty. After a visit to Texas to see his family, Chester sailed to the Phillipines as an ensign. Following cruises in the Pacific, Chester was given command of an old destroyer with orders to make it seaworthy. He managed the job so well that navy officials took special notice.

When Grandfather Karl heard that Chester had been promoted to lieutenant, he smiled and said, "My boy is on his way."

After his marriage to Catherine Freeman in 1913, Chester studied diesel engine design in Germany. During World War I, he served in submarine forces in the Mediterranean and the Atlantic. Promotions followed quickly after he helped build a submarine base in Hawaii in 1920. He was chosen to organize a Naval Reserve Officer's Training Course at the

University of California, and then to command the cruiser *Augusta* to patrol the China coast. By 1939 he was assigned to command Task Force Seven, a large group of destroyers stationed on the west coast.

When Pearl Harbor was bombed by Japanese planes on December 7, 1941, Chester Nimitz was made commander-in-chief of the Pacific. War was declared. Losses were heavy when Japanese attacked United States ships and naval and army bases.

Finally, in June 1942, the Battle of Midway was won by U.S. forces. The Japanese sea power was broken. But the Japanese continued to fight for islands that were called the "Gateway to Japan." Chester directed invasions on the Solomon Islands, Iwo Jima, Okinawa, and other places where the Japanese had hidden soldiers and ammunition.

By summer of 1944, the Japanese knew they were losing the war. In desperation they sent kamikaze pilots who dived their planes onto American ships to destroy them. They did great damage to American ships and men.

When atom bombs were dropped on Hiroshima and Nagasaki in August 1945, the Japanese surrendered. On board the USS *Missouri*, Admiral Chester Nimitz signed the peace treaty between the United States and Japan. It was September 2, 1945.

With the end of the war, Admiral Nimitz returned to the States and to his wife and four children. Special parades and tributes were given him in San Francisco, Washington, D.C., New York, Dallas, Austin, and, of course, in Fredericksburg and Kerrville.

Afterwards, he served as chief of naval operations to bring American soldiers and sailors home from the war fronts. He also was an ambassador for the United States, and made every effort to keep an honorable peace with Japan.

Invited by President Johnson to his ranch at Stonewall, Admiral Nimitz made his last trip to nearby Fredericksburg in April 1961. Once again he saw the old Steamboat Hotel, which brought back memories of his boyhood days. To the friends who had gathered to wish him well, he could only smile and say, "It's good to be home again."

Fred Gipson

1908-1973

"Something More Than a Hound-Dog Man"

Evening was story-telling time on the Gipson farm near Mason, Texas. In summer, the seven children in the family sat on the front porch of the small farmhouse to listen to tales of the frontier told by their parents. In winter, they all gathered around the fireplace, begging to hear "just one more story" before bedtime.

With his brother and five sisters, young Fred never tired of hearing about frontier days. Stories of animals, wagon trails, Indian raids, hunting and fishing—all settled into his heart and dreams.

In his early years, Fred naturally wanted to grow up to be a mule breaker and a farmer like his father. However, after several back-breaking years of picking cotton and chasing ornery mules, Fred found he was happiest while out hunting with his favorite hounds. He spent many hours tramping across familiar land as his dogs sniffed out trails of rabbits, skunks, and possums. On such days, Fred believed he had the best life possible in the Hill Country of Texas.

Fred's mother felt differently. When the hounds dug up her flower beds and carried off meat from a neighbor's smokehouse, she fretted about her son's favorite pastime.

"I have high hopes for you, Fred," she said. "I want you to grow up to be something more than a hound-dog man."

When jobs were scarce around Mason in 1933, Fred went to the University of Texas with his brother. In a freshman English class, he found he liked to write about the stories he had heard as a boy. With encouragement from his professor, he was soon writing for the school newspaper, "The Daily Texan." His gentle humor and easy flow of words won his columns many readers. They also caught the eye of a newspaper publisher in Corpus Christi. In 1937, Fred left Austin to work on the Corpus Christi Caller-Times.

Once again, newspaper readers were won over by Fred's stories of plain people and the land. Traveling around the state, he collected stories wherever he went. A column about "silly hats that women wear" drew a letter from a coed, Tommie Wynn of San Angelo. It was not long before they met and married.

When he was fired for asking for a better salary, Fred moved with Tommie back to Mason. It was time, he thought, to see if he could make a living selling stories to magazines and newspapers. Also, he was happier being close to his beloved hills where he could hunt and fish once more. "Makes a man feel like a boy again," he said.

By 1942, Fred was selling four stories a month to western magazines. More sales came when Joe Small, a friend from university days, offered to be his agent. "I'll sell the stories for you so you can have more time to write," promised Joe.

The first large sale was to *Colliers*, a national magazine, in 1943. When his story about a hound-dog man, titled "My Kind of Man," was sold to *Reader's Digest*, Fred felt he had made his fortune. Of course, the sixteen hundred dollars he received for it did not last long, especially since there would be two little sons to raise.

Fabulous Empire was the title of Fred's first book, published in 1946. It was the biography of Colonel Zack Miller, the man who had started the 101 Wild West Shows. After becoming a best-seller, it won an award from the Institute of Texas Letters.

The next book that Fred wrote, *Hound-Dog Man*, won even greater success than the first when it was published by Harpers, a New York publishing company. With money from it and from sales of *The Home Place*, Fred bought land around Mason. He had worried that farmland was being ruined by careless use. Now he planted grass and cut mesquite so that grass would have a chance to grow again.

Although his books also sold well in England and Germany, and *The Home Place* sold to movies, the next book that he wrote was a failure. Several more stories were rejected by editors, and Fred became discouraged.

Although he was hired to write a screenplay in Hollywood, Fred became so homesick for Mason that he left after three weeks. He felt he had run out of ideas, but Tommie knew better. She persuaded her husband to read books on Texas history, especially tales of Indian and pioneer life. She thought they might trigger ideas, and she was right.

Remembering a true story told to him long ago by his grandfather about a favorite yellow dog, Fred made an outline of the story and sent it to Ursula Nordstrom at Harpers. Because of her enthusiastic response, Fred and Tommie started work immediately. Within three months Tommie had finished typing Fred's story, which he called *Big Yeller Dog*. Renamed *Old Yeller*, the book became a best-seller and was made into a successful movie by Walt Disney.

Once again, Fred bought more ranch land on the Llano River. He built a house, planted bear grass in the fields, and stocked the ranch with Angus cattle. Now he could roam the land, or step out of his back door and hear the fish as they splashed in the river. He could watch flights of doves rise to the sky, and chop wood for his fireplace whenever he wanted to.

Writing at the ranch, Fred penned his last two books: *Little Arliss* and *Savage Sam*, a sequel of *Old Yeller*. Like his other writings, they held the gentle humor, the joys and sorrows of families, and the affection of simple country people for animals and for the earth that nourished their lives. In his lifetime, Fred had received these gifts with appreciation. By writing of them so well, he gave them back to readers of all ages.

Lyndon Baines Johnson

1908-1973

A Real Texan Is President

In springtime, fields of bluebonnets grew to the edge of the Pedernales River near Stonewall, Texas. Through the fields each afternoon, five-year-old Lyndon Johnson trudged from his home to his grandfather's farmhouse nearby. Sitting in a rocking chair on the porch, Lyndon's white-bearded grandfather waited for him each day. Lyndon never tired of hearing his grandfather's tales of Indian raids along the Pedernales, long cattle drives to Abilene, and dry years when no crops would grow.

"We've had a long, hard struggle making homes here in the Hill Country," said Grandfather Johnson. "Remember, Lyndon, no one in America needs to be poor. If the government makes laws to help the ordinary people, there will be enough for all."

Not long after he was five, Lyndon's family moved to Johnson City, a small town named for a distant relative. It was not easy for Lyndon to leave his grandfather and the farm. His mother, however, was glad to live in a town where there were shops, a high school, and a newspaper office.

It was his mother's hope that her oldest son would be a scholar or a lawyer and legislator, as her father had been.

But Lyndon was restless in school. He much preferred listening to his father talk with neighbors about politics, or of his years as a Texas congressman. When Lyndon was older, his father took him to meetings of the legislature in Austin.

However, when he graduated from high school in 1924, Lyndon was ready for adventure. With five other boys, he drove in a Model-T to seek his fortune in California. Fortune turned out to be odd jobs picking grapes, washing dishes, and clerking in a law office.

After two years, Lyndon went back home to Texas. For six months he worked on a road crew. It was hot, dusty, hard work. Finally he said to his parents, "I'm tired of working with my hands. I'm ready to try to make it with my brain."

After entering teacher's college at San Marcos in 1927, Lyndon worked at several odd jobs while going to school. He also wrote a column for the school paper and organized a campus political group.

Soon Lyndon attracted attention from the president of the college. President Evans made Lyndon his secretary and gave him good advice. "You are a competitor," he told Lyndon. "You can meet the challenges of the times by entering government." At the time, Lyndon was teaching Mexican-American children in Cotulla.

In 1928, Lyndon was asked to manage a state senator's campaign. He worked night and day at the job, and the campaign was won. Tall, eager Lyndon Johnson had also attracted the notice of Richard Kleberg, a Texas congressman. Kleberg invited Lyndon to be his secretary in Washington, D.C. In 1931 the young man from Johnson City went to Washington, where he was to spend the next thirty-seven years of his life.

In November 1934, after a whirlwind courtship, Lyndon married Lady Bird (Claudia) Taylor of Karnack, Texas. The next year the Johnsons returned to Austin, where Lyndon became director of the National Youth Administration in Texas. In this post he organized job education programs for young people who could not afford to go to school.

After he was elected to the House of Representatives, Lyndon and Lady Bird went back to Washington. In Congress he worked on securing a housing project for the poor in Austin, and on a bill to bring electrical power to farms and ranches in the Hill Country. It was as though he was recalling his grandfather's words: that government should meet the needs of struggling farmers and poor people.

In 1941, Lyndon was disappointed when he lost a race for the Senate. Five months later, the Japanese bombed Pearl Harbor and Lyndon joined the navy. Still a congressman, he was called back to Washington to serve in Congress until the war with Japan and Germany ended.

In 1948, Lyndon ran again for Senate. This time he won. He soon gained the position of majority leader, where he controlled the discussions of many bills.

In 1960, John Kennedy was elected president of the United States. Lyndon Johnson became vice-president. He and Lady Bird traveled to thirty-three foreign countries as ambassadors for the United States.

In November 1963, President Kennedy was assassinated in Dallas. Vice-President Johnson was immediately sworn in as president. With great dignity, he presided over the nation in a time of sorrow and confusion. He worked to continue Kennedy's plans for developing space travel, civil rights, and educational programs.

Elected to his office in 1964, President Johnson remained in the White House with Mrs. Johnson and their daughters, Luci and Lynda Bird. By working night and day, he pushed through civil rights laws for the poor and disadvantaged. He called his program "The Great Society."

War in Vietnam destroyed many of Johnson's hopes for his Great Society. The president lost favor with the nation by continuing the war even when most Americans were not in favor of it. Although he finally called a halt to the bombing, he knew he could not win another election. In 1968 he retired from politics and went back to Stonewall. There he gave his energies to running the ranch and planning a library to house his presidential papers.

At his death in 1973, President Johnson was buried in the family cemetery at Stonewall. Near him, under a huge live oak tree, are the parents and beloved grandfather who helped direct his life. The Pedernales River sparkles as it flows close by, and each spring bluebonnets come to cover the fields again.

Mildred "Babe" Didrikson
1911-1956

The "One-Woman Team" From Texas

Scrubbing floors was not a troublesome chore for young Mildred Didrikson. Tying a scrub brush on each foot, she had a fine time skating around in the foamy suds, cleaning the floor at the same time. When it came to hanging clothes out on the line, her six brothers and sisters joined in the fun. It was a race to see which one could hang the most clothes in the shortest time. Also, it was a help to their mother, who often took in washing to help support the family.

It seemed to their neighbors in Beaumont, Texas, that the Didrikson children turned everything into a game. Their backyard served as a baseball diamond much of the time. It was also a gym with a trapeze, jumping pits, a boxing ring, and weight-lifting bars made from flatirons and broomsticks. A front sidewalk was a roller-skating lane where the children raced streetcars that clanged by their house. And hedges made perfect hurdles for high-jump practice.

Leading the pack of energetic young athletes was slim, lively Mildred Didrikson. By the time she was fourteen, she was practicing in earnest, her heart set on entering the Olympic Games. They were to be held in the United States in 1932, and she wanted to be ready for them.

"All my life I've had the urge to do things better than anyone else," she declared.

That is just what she managed to do in the world of sports.

After gaining notice as a basketball player at Beaumont High School, Mildred was asked to work for an insurance company in Dallas. The company had a fine athletic program for its employees, and its teams entered many competitions. During the day, Mildred sold insurance policies. At night and on weekends, she played on the company basketball team and practiced broad jump, shot put, and jumping over hurdles. When the team won a national championship in 1931, Mildred was more sure than ever that she wanted a career in athletics.

About this time, newspaper reporters and friends gave her a nickname. They called her "Babe," after Babe Ruth, the famous baseball home-run hitter. As Babe Didrikson, Mildred gained her own fame by being "better than anyone else" in almost every sport open to women. To basketball she added the skills of javelin and discus throwing. She practiced 50-yard, 100-yard, and 200-yard dashes, broad and high jumping, and even fancy diving.

In Illinois at Northwestern University in 1932, a track-and-field meet was held for amateurs. It was Babe's first chance to compete with women athletes from all over the nation. With confidence, her coach introduced her as a "one-woman team." She astounded the whole country by winning five out of the eight events, becoming the national champion of amateur athletes.

At last Babe knew she was ready for the Olympics. They

were held in Los Angeles in July 1932. Women were allowed to enter only three events, and of course Babe entered all of them. In javelin throwing she set a world's record, and she beat the national record in the high jump event. She also won the 80-meter hurdle race.

"Ever since I was a kid, I've scrapped for everything," she told reporters. "I want to win every time."

Across the country, newspapers were full of stories about her outstanding success. When she returned to Dallas, the mayor and other town dignitaries greeted her. Thousands of people joined in a parade in her honor. It was only the beginning of even greater triumphs for Babe Didrikson.

In Los Angeles, another sports opportunity opened for her. She was invited to play the game of golf. Liking the game, she decided to concentrate on it so that she could play in tournaments. Practicing with her usual enthusiasm, Babe drove a thousand golf balls every day for a year.

In order to support herself while practicing, Babe played exhibition matches in basketball, baseball, and tennis. In some of them, men were her opponents. Still working half-days at the insurance company, she practiced golf swings from 5:30 to 8:30 each morning, and from 3:30 until dark each evening. At night she studied the rules of golf and played her harmonica for fun.

As a professional, Babe also made tours of Australia and the United States. Another financial help was a contract with a sporting goods company. Her picture appeared in advertisements for their products.

At a golf match in Los Angeles, Babe met George Zaha-

102

rias, a young professional wrestler. When George drove his golf ball farther down the fairway than Babe's, she took an immediate liking to him. They were married in December 1938. After the move to Denver to make their home, George began to promote Babe's career as a golfer. Babe also took an active part in the community. She taught baseball, golf, and swimming classes to children in orphanages and detention homes.

From 1945 to 1947, Babe won seventeen golf tournaments in a row. Crowds followed her around the golf links, not only to see her play but also to hear the funny things she said. The same thing happened when she played in Scotland for the British Women's Amateur title in 1947. She not only won the title, she also won the hearts of the British people with her fun-loving spirit.

When she returned home by boat, she was met by her husband with seventy reporters in New York. In Denver, the mayor gave her a key to the city, and ten thousand people came to cheer her in a colorful parade.

Babe continued playing golf and teaching at the Chicago Country Club as a pro. Together, Babe and George established The Ladies' Professional Golf Association. She also starred in short movies about golf, wrote a newspaper column, and authored a book titled *Championship Golf*.

Winning ninety-two medals in her lifetime, Babe was named by the Associated Press Club as "The Woman Athlete of the Half Century" in 1950. It seemed she would never stop winning.

However, the greatest battle of her life came when it was

learned that she had cancer. With her usual confident spirit, Babe said, "All my life I've been competing and competing to win. I came to realize that, in its way, cancer was the toughest competition I'd faced yet. I determined to come back and win just as before."

A few months after an operation, she was back on the golf course and won two matches. In spite of pain and weakness, she gave radio and television talks in behalf of cancer education. With her husband, she established the Babe Didrikson Fund to support clinics and treatment centers for cancer patients.

During the last days of her illness, Babe asked to be taken from the hospital to the golf links so that she could touch the green turf once again. Her appreciation for the sports that had meant so much to her never left her memory. She and George established a trophy to be given each year to the woman athlete in the United States who has done the most for amateur sports. The trophy forms a visible tie from Babe to athletes of the future. She will be remembered by everyone as a great woman who brought her talents, strengths, and enthusiasm to the world of sports.

Barbara Jordan

1936-1996

Strong Voice for the Constitution

"You can be different," said Grandfather Patten to his five-year-old granddaughter. "You just trot your own horse and don't get in the same rut as everyone else."

Her grandfather's words were important to Barbara Jordan. Listening to him during Sunday visits was the highlight of each week for her. Together they talked as they sorted rags and old newspapers for Grandfather Patten's junkyard business in downtown Houston.

In the evening he read to Barbara by the light of the kerosene lamp. She heard passages from the Bible, poetry, hymns, and word definitions from Webster's Dictionary. She memorized many of the readings and repeated them to her grandfather. The one she recited most often was his favorite.

> "Just remember, the world is not a playground, but a schoolroom. Life is not a holiday, but an education. One eternal lesson for us all: to teach us how better we should love."

As a child, Barbara gave little thought to what her grandfather meant by "being different." She liked things the way they were. Her days were spent riding her bicycle and playing with school friends. On Sundays she went to church services and sang with her parents and two sisters in the choir. In school and church programs, she was often asked to recite poems and read stories. People liked to listen to the strong, deep tones of her voice and the lively way in which she spoke.

Not until Barbara went to Phillis Wheatley High School did she begin to understand what being different could mean. She became aware that schoolmates, church friends, neighbors — all of them were black, as she and her family were.

"Why is it," she wondered, "that black students go to one school and white students go to another? Do we learn the same things? How will we ever meet?"

All over the United States, people were asking the same questions. In 1950 these questions were brought before the Supreme Court of the United States because of the Sweatt v. Painter case. A young black man, Heman Sweatt, claimed that he had not been allowed to enter the University of Texas Law School because of the color of his skin. University officials had told him that there were schools for blacks where he could get a law degree. But Heman argued that black schools could not offer the same quality of education as white schools. To be fair, public schools should be integrated, or open to everyone. Segregation is against the law, he claimed, because the Constitution says that all Americans should have equal opportunities. With the help of a lawyer, Mr. Sweatt brought suit against President Painter of the University of Texas.

When Barbara heard of the case, she became deeply

interested in the idea of integration. On the school debate team she argued for it so well that she attracted notice from teachers and students.

After winning local and national awards in high school for her skill in debating, Barbara was determined to become a lawyer. She knew she would have to excel in her studies and learn to speak well before large groups of people.

Winning a scholarship, Barbara entered all-black Texas Southern University in Houston. The speech coach there recognized her abilities as a speaker and a student. Barbara gained confidence as her coach helped her to sharpen her thinking, speak more clearly, and defend her ideas. Competing with debaters from other schools, she became an outstanding speaker.

After graduation with highest honors, Barbara went to Boston University to study for a law degree. In the meantime, the Supreme Court had ruled that schools for blacks were not equal to schools for whites. After the ruling, schools across the country were opened to people of all races and backgrounds.

After receiving a law degree, Barbara returned to Houston and opened a private law practice. Because she was eager to take part in government, she also entered politics. During the Kennedy-Johnson presidential campaign, she urged black neighborhoods to vote for their rights. By speaking at schools, churches, and civic clubs, she succeeded in getting blacks of Harris County to go to the polls.

As her interest in politics grew, Barbara was urged to run for the Texas House of Representatives. Twice she entered races of the House, but each time she lost. "I found out I didn't like losing, Barbara said. "I determined it wouldn't happen again."

In 1966 Barbara ran for the Texas Senate. Winning the race, she became the first black woman elected to the Texas Legislature. As Senator Jordan, she ably served on state committees. She gained the respect of voters and senators alike.

In the fall of 1972, Texas elected Barbara Jordan to the United States House of Representatives. She moved to Washington, D.C. and became the first black woman from the South to be a member of Congress.

There she worked to pass laws that would help the poor, the disadvantaged, and the average citizen. Honors came to her because of her dedication. Among these are an honorary doctorate from Harvard University, the role of keynote speaker for the Democratic Convention in 1976, and being named to the Texas Women's Hall of Fame.

In 1978 Senator Jordan returned to Austin, Texas. She became a professor at the LBJ School of Public Affairs at the University of Texas. Her interest in politics and law remained keen.

When Senator Jordan died in January 1996, she was buried in the State Cemetery in Austin among other great Texans. She will be remembered as one who helped lead the way to a better life for all Americans.

Glossary

accomplishment — an ability, quality or skill gained by training or practice.

accuracy — freedom from mistake or error.

admiral — a high-ranking officer in the navy.

adopt — to accept formally and put into effect.

amateur — a person who takes part in sports for pleasure and not for pay.

ambassador — an official agent of good will between countries.

ancestor — a person from whom one is descended, and who lived in a much earlier time.

appoint — to officially name to a position.

arbor — a shelter made of vines or branches twisted together.

archive — a place in which public records or historical documents are stored.

astound — to amaze or surprise.

attire — clothing.

ballad — a song that tells a story and has many short verses.

barge — a broad, flat-bottomed boat.

betray — to be unfaithful or treacherous to.

billow — to bulge or swell out through wind action.

biography — a written history of a person's life.

bloomers — full, loose trousers gathered at the knee.

bookkeeping — the keeping of business and financial records by entering them in books.

botany — a branch of life science dealing with plants.

breed — a group of similar, related animals.

cavalry — an army of soldiers on horseback.

charter — an official statement in writing by an authority or government, outlining the rights and duties of the society that receives it.

chisel — a metal tool used to shape or chip away stone; to cut or shape with a chisel.

civic — having to do with a citizen, a city, or a city's affairs.

civilizer — one who helps to develop a culture.

110

clash — to come into conflict.

classify — to arrange into classes or groups.

clinic — a hospital where patients are treated and medical instruction takes place.

colony — a distant territory belonging to a nation.

column — a special department appearing in a newspaper.

compass — a device that shows direction by means of a magnetic needle that turns to point north on a dial.

compete — to try to do something as well as or better than another person.

covenant — a solemn and binding promise in writing.

custom — a habit or practice common to a person or people.

debate — a formal discussion of a question in which arguments for opposing points of view are presented.

debt — something that is owed.

degree — the status given to a student by a college or professional school after a program of study is completed.

descent — one's relationship by birth to one's ancestors.

desperation — a state of hopelessness leading to recklessness or panicked action.

destroyer — a small, fast warship armed with guns and other weapons.

detention — temporary confinement.

develop — to go through a process of natural or gradual growth.

dictator — a person who rules with absolute power and who is often cruel or oppressive.

dignitary — a person of high position or honor.

disadvantaged — poor, unemployed, or without rights.

discus — a disk that is hurled for distance as a sport.

dismay — alarm or disappointment.

doctorate — the degree, title, or rank of a doctor.

document — an original or official piece of paper containing information or proof of something.

donate — to make a gift of.

empire — all the territory held by one country or power.

encouragement — help in the form of supportive words or actions.

enforce — to carry out effectively.

escort — to go along with in order to protect.

eternal — everlasting.

excel — to surpass others.

exhibition — a public showing.

extract — something withdrawn by a chemical or physical process.

fertile — capable of producing much plant growth.

financial — having to do with money.

freight — something that is loaded for transportation.

furrow — a trench in the earth made by a plow.

garrison — a military post.

grant — the transfer of property.

gristmill — a mill for grinding grain.

guidance — the act or process of guiding.

harvest — to gather in a crop.

hostile — behaving as an enemy; extremely unfriendly.

immigrant — a person who comes to a country to live permanently.

inspire — to influence, move, or guide by good example.

institute — an organization for the study of a certain field.

insurance — a contract by which one party guarantees another against loss.

insurance policy — a specific set of conditions under which one party guarantees another against loss.

integrated — united with something else.

invasion — the entrance of an army into a country for conquest.

invention — something produced for the first time through imagination or experiment.

javelin — a spear-like metal shaft that is thrown for distance in a field event.

kerosene — an oil derived from petroleum that is used as a fuel.

learned — having knowledge gained through study.

legislator — a person who makes laws as part of a committee.

legislature — a committee of people having the power to make laws.

lever — a bar used for prying or dislodging something.

lilt — a lively, springy manner.

lore — a body of knowledge that is taught or learned.

112

maxim — a rule of conduct.

militia — the whole body of citizens subject to call to military service.

minority — a group that is smaller in number than other groups, or that is not in power, or does not have full rights.

missionary — a person on a religious mission.

motto — a sentence or phrase expressing a guiding principle.

naturalist — a field biologist.

odds — chances or probability.

opponent — one that takes an opposite position (as in a debate, contest, or conflict).

ornery — having an irritable disposition.

pallet — a mattress.

pantaloons — close-fitting trousers with straps passing under the foot.

pastime — something that makes time pass pleasantly.

patriot — one who loves his or her country.

persevere — to carry on in spite of discouragement or opposition.

persuade — to urge successfully to change a belief or course of action.

philosophy — the study of man's principles, beliefs, and knowledge.

pioneer — a person who goes first in some activity, opening new ways; one of the first to settle an area.

plantation — a farming settlement worked by hired laborers.

political — having to do with a government.

poll — a place where votes are cast in an election.

portion — a part of a whole.

process — to make into a product by means of a special treatment.

prosperous — successful.

protestor — one who complains, objects, or shows unwillingness.

province — a part of a country, or a country under the control of another country.

quarry — to dig or take from the ground.

rebel — one who goes against authority.

reform — change of what is bad or wrong.

republic — a government made up of elected leaders.

resent — to have ill will over.

resign — to give up an office or position.

retreat — the withdrawal of troops.

reveal — to make known.

scarce — not plentiful.

scholar — a learned person.

scholarship — a grant of funds to a student in order to pay for his or her education.

sculptor — one who creates sculptures by modeling materials into works of art.

segregated — separated by races.

settle — to establish a home in.

somber — serious or grave.

specimen — a sample.

stampede — a wild rush of frightened animals.

stockman — one who works in the raising of livestock.

suit — an action taken in a court of law to enforce a right or claim.

survey — to determine the form, size, and position of a piece of land.

surveyor — one who surveys.

suspect — to believe to be true; to believe in the guiltiness of.

terraqueous — having to do with both land and water.

territory — a geographical area belonging to a government.

thesis — an original research paper with a central topic or point of view.

thicket — a thick growth of small trees, shrubbery, or underbrush.

thong — a strip of leather used for fastening.

treaty — an agreement between governments.

tribute — a gift or act showing respect, gratitude, or affection.

undertake — to take upon oneself as a task.

vast — very great in size, amount, degree, or extent.

volunteer — one who offers his services of his own free will.

yodel — to sing as if shouting or calling, with sudden change in pitch.

zeal — eagerness.

Printed in the United States
2677